Hills full of holes

poems

Dan Alter

Fernwood
PRESS

Hills full of holes

©2025 by Dan Alter

Fernwood Press
Newberg, Oregon
www.fernwoodpress.com

All rights reserved. No part may be reproduced
for any commercial purpose by any method without
permission in writing from the copyright holder.

Printed in the United States of America

Cover and page design: Mareesa Fawver Moss
Cover art: Ross Belot
Author photo: Adrianne Mathiowetz

ISBN 978-1-59498-157-9

For Hadas—
I'll always share a trail with you

Trying to heal from a concussion, Dan Alter walks the parkland trails and hills of the East Bay, day after day. The poems he composes on his walks echo other walkers—Frost, Yeats, Thoreau—but also weave a new and plangent music of longing and mourning, rooting and wandering, of repair and unraveling. Amid crow-scrape and ant-data, Alter explores a landscape of ghosts and historic violence, of memory and erasure. "Please Mr. Wind reshuffle me," he writes, but his poems reshuffle us, too.

—TESS TAYLOR
author of *Rift Zone* and *Work & Days*

Beguiling. Bewildering. Beautiful. Foreboding. *Hill Full of Holes*, Dan Alter's multivalent, musical collection of poems, evokes our planet's majesty and peril as developers bulldoze forests and birds seek new migration patterns: "The sky turns/ its back on us but we/ can't tell because it's/ also blue." Recovering from a traumatic brain injury, our poet hikes trails in the woods and hills overing the East Bay in California, seeking to read the world or have the world read him. Our speaker seeks remedy in birds whose calls he does not know, "almost neon/ in the canopy/ what time is/ it they/ keep saying." Gerard Manley Hopkins who wept when trees were cut, Thoreau who fixed Walden Pond like an eye on the world, Frost who stopped in the woods, and novelist Richard Powers who sings of our mistakes rattle and comfort throughout these poems. If you love the earth, are calmed by walks in the forest, need nature to thrive, then place these gentle poems by your bedside. Though rapacious early explorers, contemporary money mongers, and ongoing climate change have carved holes in our world, these poems' lyrical witness will leave you whole.

—SPENCER REECE
an Episcopal priest and author of
The Clerk's Tale and *The Road to Emmaus*

Subtle, spare poems, many of them set in the hiking trails above Berkeley, California, expand into a book that examines the land as an extension of our physical selves, our journey through physical space and also excavating the layers of history, conquest, and urban development. These immersive poems open interior and exterior worlds and diminish dichotomies of plant and human, nature and industry, history and now. Tender and vivid, these poems ask the reader to change perspectives and see the world anew.

—JUDY HALEBSKY
author of *Spring and a Thousand Years* and *Tree Line*

Contents

Loop I: please mister wind 11
Wind opens me closed 12
I fell 13
Butterfly hidden in hills color 14
No returns 15
Taking cane 16
Westward Frank C Havens 17
Sweet little 18
Whose woods 19
In the middle of 20
Poem with time & mildly injured brain 21
You said 22
Blue 23
Whose woods 24
In a last 25
Because my father got a better job 26
Ripples 28
Who goes 29
Off trail 30

Chaparral ("the understory") ... 31
Whose woods ... 32
Every day the same ... 33
Days unshowered ... 34
Whose woods ... 35
Greenness with picnic bench ... 36
You sleep ... 38
Whose woods ... 39
Poem in blue with the news ... 40
"What fish feel" ... 41
Ode to fMRI (the Cure) ... 42
Whose woods ... 44

Loop II: sky turns its back on us ... 45
Stony trail, visibility nil ... 46
Whose woods ... 47
David won't call me from his car anymore ... 48
Manzanita barren ... 49
Across grazing hills ... 50
Whose woods ... 51
Whose woods ... 52
How can I ... 53
Does the bay ... 55
Hills full of holes ... 56
Birds I don't know ... 57
Whose woods ... 58
For a worker in song ... 59
Infinity approximates as a canyonful of leaves ... 60
On waves ... 61
On the hinge ... 62
What's my ... 65
Whose woods ... 66
Bounced back no forwarding ... 67
How much fire ... 68

Are you coming to the farewell party 70
Brain-ache at San Leandro Creek 71
Poem for a watershed with found objects 72
Whose woods 74
Could I 75
Greenness with picnic bench 76

Note on the poems 79
Sources 81
Acknowledgments 83
Title Index 85
First Line Index 89

Loop I:
please mister wind

Wind opens me closed

Birdcall a doorlatch
          I go through
     I'm through   again

Tilden

I fell

      apart on a little wind
                      all day   ridge wind
          whoosh in the high pines

Above cul-de-sacs I
      slumped out of noise that was
                  a plane going
          over
          my leg came tiny
     lining ants
              a trunk
         I didn't fit
             a self   I tried
        to feel more like
                 a leaf while
  hush
       flooded entirely
up the canyon

Pine stand above Curran Tr @ Meadows Canyon Tr

Butterfly hidden in hills color

O common buckeye on the ground
or stitched to wind: dirt-shaded
door to 450 million years,
I didn't know. Crows
play their scrapers, ants increase
their data, on my single
footpath I found out:
how you are another here,
hills beiged. Your purple
eyespots glow like lamps
in cannabis, stare
like the price of gas.
A California, combustible,
party where the earth
comes apart. I looked you up,
you were glued to US letters,
24 cents. Gray pulse
I put away. On my table you
were the knife left
untouched. Months
I walked room to room
in hills blown through by wind
full of machines,
moving. My shoe soles molded
in China, while you worked
on four furry wings lightly
as parentheses, ancestors
having aimed you at nectar
in the yellow flowers before
they reach the change.

No returns

I went into the outlet store
even though it was bad
for my head. Gleaming
tined music people
grabbing through the racks.
Samples, 25%. Found
about what I wanted
though not as many pockets.
Lines, inserted chip
signed when she said.
Everyone moving their hands
too fast through bins. Cars
going everywhere
too slowly. Mine
went too slowly
& too fast
until at trailhead
I loaded up the new
backpack at last
big enough & walked in.

Northface/Quarry Tr.

Taking cane

                              of twisty
                  Australian branch in hand
                        onto trail
                                  upturns
                     lizard skitter
        sad sack
                              trees drooping
                     over thistlefields

        Whose woods
                  are these

                        East it's all ruin-
                                  brown hills thatched
                  with roof & surly evergreen

                                  Up here   air whisper
                     on a rock   thimble brown
                              bird-flicker

                     Whose woods
        not Fergus's   no voice of a fire-
                        forked pine

                                            Worn
                  footpaths   walk me

Seaview Tr.

Westward Frank C Havens

       highborn of Sag Harbor came
put his hands on the manifestations of money as it was fluxing
through laws stocks banks possession of lands. In his mansion's
opium room dabbled in meditation planned to own every
ungrasped acre of hill east of Oakland. Hills where for was it a
 hundred
centuries people had burnt grassland to keep back woods.
Where Spanish cattle-hooves scattered ryegrass seeds wild oats
foxtail uniforming the hills a grazing brown. Now his
"People's Water Company" bought up all
the watershed you could walk in a dried summer's day.

      In 1910 began planting Tasmanian
blue gum seedlings river red gum shipped from the bottom
of the world paid his men a nickel per, in four years
millions across the creek-running hills. Their stunning growth rate
looked just liked money. Eucalyptus coppices: they would never
need to replant. The brochure hosanna'd *telegraph poles* to *violins*,
railway sleepers to *insulator pins*. But planed

it chipped, cracked when dried. Four years: nurseries
& sawmill shuttered. Matrices of what had been Frank
dispersed into nothing from which comes the thought.

        Southbound monarchs
nest in stands his money left. Wind creaks
in & out. Straggly branch scatter bark heaps.
Brain-tired no place to lie down.
My own strangeness a taste I can't spit out.

Sweet little

    switchback
        Winded
     eucalyptus doorcreak
  From triple-height
    yellow   fingerleaves
          falling
  like the cloud
 covered light
    on a gust

I'm sorry
    sore cortex
      are you
    still fraying

Where the creek
   pools water skeeters
    pause
  on four
    pontoons
     Gnatswirl
      halfway
   over trickle

Ferny feelers
      laurel leaf-paddles
     float forward
    Chlorophyll hued
     proliferate shade
    in woods we have
      set aside glowing

Laurel Canyon Trail

Whose woods

> November 1826

The number of wild geese ... is quite extraordinary, and indeed would hardly be credited by anyone who had not seen them covering whole acres of ground, or rising in myriads with a clang that may be heard at a considerable distance. They are said to arrive in California in November, and to remain there until March.

In the middle of

        a lot of sky
     I'm coming
          toward a stray cloud
before noon loose
    in air   chased up
     from stucco   cursive
         beer-signs glass
      not glowing

What was the name
        of that mothy
   color-splotched
     four wings

        From the far valley
    mushrooms
       music   wavering
          away from its hinges   in the middle

of my life
       it's footpath miles   over mild
     Novemberhills   to get to my daughter's
  last bell

oh I don't
    want to be late

Belgium Tr.

Poem with time & mildly injured brain

```
        Spidery night: sleep webby        day laced with thinner
than visible gaps                later that morning         an aura
        or the air like water        green pieces
of seeing break         into grains:        more weeks        go

        to office after office        from walls a hollow
flute lulls        meridians slight-needled
        neckbone        probed        or gazed into
with swivel        whirr:        worry a skullcap to keep not
        taking off                trying for miles
to heal by root-web        grass sway

        Slow leaked:  the spin        & balance on which life
wheeled:                concussion        echoes on        its how many
                times a hundred no's:        many voices        splinter
in an exposed ceiling                        headlights
        blade:                month wears

into months        foil halo of ache again        a stuck
        from inside door:        outside        I drift        neurons
from a million years                give up in green
        seconds:        light leaves a pine that fell
a little at a time                is that circling
        birds                or what's caught from
a song        that I forget the words
```

You said

                there were no more
frozen blueberries. There were.
I said so. You were staring
at them. Right there
I said a few times. But how
I sounded. You
said about how. I said
back. At that point

the whole thing was over.
        In Greenland more

ice shelf   calved
                Rain   went farther away
     from our coast   Huge
             beige   beetles spread
in the grazing hills   glistening
             like insides out
     You   took her to school   I began
             my day waist deep in it

Mezzue @ San Pablo Ridge Trs.

Blue

    sun blaring   my eyes
        Please mister wind
            reshuffle me

Mezzue @ San Pablo Ridge Trs.

Whose woods

                                        November 1826

    of wild
                        indeed   *hardly*
anyone   *covering*   *acres*
or rising
        a clang   *a*
distance   *They*   *said*   *in California*

In a last

                    corner   brown
clouds of redwoods drift
     their theory
from a long way
        Light gets older   auburns
rusted greens   shy
       away from it in closets
of shade I will
       lie down in

Itinerant fly
      faint bird
chitter   air slowed
      to near zero

On far-up thread
      sun columns
Specks of bright
      circulate on how
tiny wings

Starflower Tr.

Because my father got a better job

                    a hundred & some years
after men as if there were not
words for each of its mosses
       had gutted the forest
of coastal oak & ballooned
their one- or two-stories
across the plain

                         we
arrived in the tide
of west-moving vans
to leafy streets named for seizers
of parcels a news-
paper baron a bear stirring
only on nylon

the weather was so gentle
all-morning fog hung
around like ghost friends
who would in a whisper
sing along after
their fog dinner parties
       the highway
was like a young
confident president
& there was a richer
blend of coffee to nurse
on the corner of Oxford
& Vine when my always
looking up father

brought us to Berkeley's
stucco slopes   it seemed
like a perfect idea

                 who knew the concrete
footings we asked
a bank for were poured
on top of dances

Ripples

        where water   skeeters paddle
                the pool
pulses spilled
                    circles   (later the word
      comes back   *concentric*)
                                    of something
        a lot like light

Laurel Creek Tr.

Who goes

                      into the dry dry
          hills on a dust   rocks
                fire-road so sun
  exposed
                      Joggers
terrier-walkers
              ladyfriends   loud talk
      half-liter in hand

                    & me in
            trouble above the shoulders

                      In the laureltops
          a breeze barely trying   loose ends
  of skinny birdcalls   a fly
        zig zags   faceward

Was that a hawk
          low russet swoop
     sorry for your   no name
          in my poem

Where the trail widens
          back to one rattle-down
    lane I am some bones
     & skin in the open

Round Top Loop Tr.

Off trail

              I tumbled almost
down broomy scrub
      sock-stick to a shade-
abandoned tire

When the hands-on doctor
      presses the casing
of my worry for minutes
      it changes to more like
a lake

      Pine-
needle litter
            I'm in
     a brittle

birdscribble crescendo

Seaview Tr.

Chaparral ("the understory")

                        Coyote brush
Blackberry   Hazelnut
      Snowberry
                  Toyon
Wild currant
        Hounds' tongue
                    Sword fern   Wood fern
        Fairy bells
     Woodland star
                 Alum root
        Angelica

List of vegetation in the East Bay Regional Parks, from a trail sign

Whose woods

November 1792

We had not proceeded far from this delightful spot, when we entered a country I little expected to find in these regions. For about twenty miles it could only be compared to a park, which had originally been closely planted with the old English oak; the underwood, that had probably attended its early growth, had the appearance of having been cleared away, and had left the stately lords of the forest in complete possession of the soil, which was covered with luxuriant herbage, and beautifully diversified with pleasing eminences and vallies; which, with the range of lofty rugged mountains that bounded the prospect, required only to be adorned with the neat habitations of an industrious people, to produce a scene not inferior to the most studied effect of taste in the disposal of grounds ...

Every day the same

                        branch   rustle
            motorcycle savaging
canyon air like it's theirs

                Stray glint
                                spider-threads
  Green-bellied
                bottle-flies want
          something
                at the edges of where I put things
                            together   I fail & lie
        on leaves again

Never saw
                that movie where a man
     eats faces   What fantasy
              are we slowly
    losing in
            Watch ticking only
              an idea
              in its chip   The doctor
that's not until
              December probably can't
    help anyway

        Into silence   I'm making
              one more   withdrawal

Willow Tr.

Days unshowered

with Basho

                                        busy pin-flies
do I smell
              like dying
         What voice
in a slight breeze   stalks
         leaves on a sapling
laurel   all
        trembling
from seven months'
        not rain we get
no relief

        Not this human sadness
but baked dry oakleaves on
        a nameless hill

jetroar & trainhorn blender
        both sides of sky

        Bird-swirl
in near trees   This sparse
        shade   not changing
mind   *attached to nothing*
       by my face   the razor
whine of suffering

Pine Tree Tr.

Whose woods

                                                                       November 1792

                   far   *we entered*
                                                only
                                    the   *English*
              appearance   *cleared away*
    lords of

          lofty   *required only*

       disposal

Greenness with picnic bench

for Tilden park

Elaborate gnat & dapple, O Tilden
you honky-tonk set-aside we come
on four wheels & two. Muddy switchback,
casual horse-road, you merry-go-round
concession, fenceful of show-farm
goats. Gor-Texed we come to you,
all day our days have waited
like our dogs. Our days behind walls.

Go to the back of the line mountain lion,
recede with coyote & nut gatherer,
we've stood a grill on steel pole,
we've riveted weather for squirrel,
opened door for poison oak. We've left
on streambanks our single-use
beverage cups. Piñatas have been burst,
reprieve given to pent-up dogs.

Tilden you tale of a land sandwich,
acres we say escape. O sew
the thread lightly, great bobbin & needle
of development, attach this last parcel
of oak-bay & toyon, even if corrupted
with long sloppy trees that came on boats:
we have dogs, we have pockets awash
with code. We are extending summer
like a bridge span, our commute
ravenous, our nights bedazzled,
please don't leave us.

Keep patching together ants
& undergrowth. Wild raspberry,
a few poppies soldiering. Memory-stapled
trails. Don't leave yet:
your hair full of wind.

You sleep

                     with our daughter
down the hall
                  Last night before
I hid from how light
        hurts I smelled something appley
you heated

       Three a.m.   Am I passing
by every
        chance at being
happy

A few rolling
        tires   carry hours
left of darkness   through a window cracked
        the wrong way
Unmoving
        clouds patch sky
the underside of white

California St.

Whose woods

August 6, 1775

At this cove ... there is a rancheria of Indians, who came out from their huts shouting and gesticulating to our men to come ashore. With the intention of taking soundings our men went a short way toward land, and on seeing this the Indians set up at the shore's edge a pole with a bunch of feathers at the top. Not being instructed to respond, our men kept well away; but the Indians, no doubt thinking it was mistrust that made them do so, sought to lessen it by throwing their bows to the ground and, first waving them round in the air, sticking all their arrows in the sand.

Poem in blue with the news

         Even if it's not
   a flower
moss is can I say   blooming
     on the fallen
   Monterey   pine limbs

     Motors   go burning   up the world

     Dylan won
  the prize   today   that is made
     from explosives   in Sweden
I look for his
    song but the words
   crumble
            Sunlight comes late
     to the party & leaves
   again   The wind my
     actual friend returns
  to tell me what
    I can't say

Where the evidence I
    try to assemble
       thins   tree shadows
   patch   up the hillside
   Zippery flies reckon
      with something not
   visible   in pineneedle dirt

Willow Tr.

"What fish feel"

with Basho

                    in a cold ocean
why is it not
                what I feel in the end
      of November deep
shade of closed-cone pines
        it's not like anything

        a blowfly's zigzags
footsteps up the hill
        sun at three already feels
like going down

This road—
        faint grass beside
mud also coming
        back downhill
a few miles from where
        everyone is driving
almost to my door

Panoramic Tr.

Ode to fMRI (the Cure)

& this is for the core, bathed
in helium, from which oscillates
the field, my head inside
its science: we have seized portions
of the universe, attached to them
terms. *F* is for *functional*.
Poem for the enameled
metal donut whirr din
buzz through facebones, something
called a halo exciting hydrogen
in blood which does or doesn't
move through convolutes as I
pursue word strings
sent in by mirror.
M for *magnetic*.
Resonance is the *R*. Ode
to technology applied at an oblique
angle, glass-front clinic
in Utah visited by men
whose brains have ricocheted
in stadiums. By those
who stayed too long at a table
of fog. Poem
for Provo, friendly Mormons
tailoring cures out of *imaging*,
I. For the soft-
spoken driver of a car
sideswiped in Toronto,
two shy students & the Denver
fast-food eater falling
on his head since he could walk. All

remembering in order twenty
picture cards, alphabet
backwards, buttons
flashing at our fingers, a feel almost
of burning as re-synapsed
blood flows back. Icicle
branches over Provo River,
snowy Wasatch Range,
its theaters Sundance watching.
Four letters, three phases,
maybe a million dollars. This

is for how many human hours
until there were superconductors
swimming in a cryostat,
shim cools smoothing
fluxes of what they call
field, images culled
by coils named gradient. Wheels
of sine waves in which rests
a riddle, a head. Readout
screen. January, Provo
River rushing through ice.

Whose woods

August 6, 1775

who came   *shouting*

toward land   *taking*

    the edge   *feathers*

      to lessen

all their arrows   *sand*

Loop II:
sky turns its back on us

Stony trail, visibility nil

Fog pours
      it rains from branches
that came from Monterrey
      Needle rusted the
fire road winds
      into whiteout

Why did you
      lie down here runt
raccoon with flies your fur
      pine-needled
eyes blanked open

Seaview Tr.

Whose woods

April 1806

It was then a perfect calm, and in a very fine morning we commenced our return to St. Francisco. The channel which we followed to get into the bay was full of sea-otters and sea-dogs; many lay on the muddy shores, and others were swimming with their heads just above the water ... [O]ur stomachs were so craving for food, that we renounced all the joys and advantages which might have been derived from the chase of these animals ... Three sea-otters, however, who lay sleeping almost close to our boat, presented a temptation not to be resisted, and these we did kill and carry away with us.

David won't call me from his car anymore

     Lazing in striations
                of shaded water
streaked by sun leaning   away

                    Cityward
          an ex-dock's dotted
                line of posts & broken roadtop

O weedy grass at the end
                of land
          speckled pause
      & dart ground squirrels
                          you don't say
         a thing about David's no more
                    messages

     For no reason
          now camera-ready
    a path of brighter
            water
                    Through tide-out
                    sludge
    gulls picking

             half-sunk   tires
                  even a stranded
    traffic cone

Ceasar Chavez Park Perimeter Tr.

Manzanita barren

                with bird-seeded
huckleberry slowly
       taking over   across Skyline from lookout
homes on stilts
     cold air follows me

From electrodes on my scalp trying
      to shake five
months gravel out of gray
     folds I
drive to hilltop
      the same truck & walk
into birdland

In low-tide cloudlight
      on a stone bench I'm
fading with names
      from trail signs
snowberry sword fern
     madrone

Huckleberry Path

Across grazing hills

with Gerard Manley Hopkins

        like a robot wind
all day
    blows the banded noise
      of us moving

      Nailed to a little oak
I found a plaque
    inscribed   *I have desired to go*

  I have heard god
    loves me
but feel more like an empty
      in the pushy hillwind

            Where springs not fail
Grinding
flour from my
    own warm bones
at 1:30 woke to worry
    which doctors & how

        To fields
Is it always the same time
    in the freeway's
    rebar spine
           where flies no sharp and sided hail
    The hills die in very slow
    motion so many shades
of empty   blond   brown   wan
           And a few lilies blow
Belgium Tr.

Whose woods

>   April 1806

>   *so craving for*
>   *advantages*
>   *these animals*
>   *we   carry with us*

Whose woods

October 8, 1769

... besides the many good-sized cottonwoods on the river, there begins here a large mountain range covered with a tree very like the pine in its leaf, save that this is not over two fingers long; the heartwood is red, very handsome wood, handsomer than cedar ... There are great numbers of this tree here, of all sizes and thickness, most of them exceedingly high and straight like so many candles: what a pleasure to see this blessing of timber.

How can I

      sing the misery whip, a man at each end as its crosscut
         teeth tore
on the draw, on the push. The maul, ten pound sledge, steel
  wedges
kept the long blade from binding. Things they called cant hook,
grapple & chain for oxen to drag giant auburn logs away.
  Sing a forest

older than Jesus, nine steam-, one water-powered saw mills,
  in ten years
nothing but stumps. With trail-joggers & Steller's jays
  I have also soaked
in the slow time of their orphans, baby *Sequoia Sempervirens*,
  not knowing
how the park sprouted back from clearcut, twice.
  Twice: my eyes open

at three a.m. Too early or too late to make a song,
  of a lucky patch of fog in hills, trees so tall
that by them the clippers steered clear of underwater rock
  called Blossom. Sing
greed, sing gold, men surged in from Oregon & Maine, China,
  Mexico,
French fleeing revolutions, by wagon, steamship, generations
of hunger smoldering in their bones. Little Yerba Buena remade

in the frenzy San Francisco. Remaining tribes bounty-hunted,
  squatted out,
starved, how much more greed than gold, & all those settlers
needing houses. On your postcard ride up Powell Street
by cable car, can you hear the ache of its redwood skeleton?
  Of wood

that after death keeps giving, lack of resins passing it
even through fire. Sing a very sad song of Oakland
raised up from backwater port, Park Boulevard, Redwood Road
descending past the room where my daughter was born,
arteries laid from logging camp to docks where
    floorboards shipped;

of the university founded near clearcut, which would put decades
of handmade bread on my father's table. Where I sit & eat. I pan
for my lines in stump fields, listen for the crack of a
    400-foot tree falling,
inside freeway roar our true river, in my early morning tunnel,

no sleep again. My mind times out on all the talking
that happened in old-growth, information fluting through
    mycelial thread,
scent. Tree ghosts, what do you say now while you keep out rain
& wind above our faces to screens. When the mills closed down,

there was only one left. At 93 feet, a runt tree angling
    from cliffside,
not worth the trouble. I'm thinking of the giant
    California condor
no longer nesting, shy understory of redwood sorrel
    & wake robin
bye bye. I'm not sleeping, I'm thinking of two men

pulling a 16-foot saw blade called misery to
& fro through an ancient base, their pores exuding
    alcohol. Putting
as we do food on table. Of their misery versus the tree's.

Does the bay

        forgive us   Giant-banked

            clouds bus south

Our windows

            where the big shadow

    slides off   flash

        Between two shores

            of glitter floats

the slower process we

    call water From here

            I hear crows & always

  the falling

            off the world sound
      of our going

    Myself driven

        a million miles

Sirens & sparrowcalls

off Mezzue Tr.

Hills full of holes

                      the wind hollows   it is
      bigger   like everyone I
              wait for the data
to load   Here
              fallen pine limbs disintegrate
      casually   In needles
            & leaning branches
                  comes sunlight
            The far valley hovers
                    evergreen & new grass

      You gone   rainclouds roll
back   Coyote brush & oak go
      down to the creek surging
            deep in canyon
      shade   We did so many
        things for an idea
we had about love

Skyline Tr.

Birds I don't know

        their calls

                almost neon

   in the canopy

           what time is

  it they

      keep saying

        a door in the moment

   I sit on a slope

break waiting for

Chown & French Trs.

Whose woods

August 24, 1775

    They all crowded around me and, sitting by me, began to sing, with an accompaniment of two rattles that they had brought with them. As they finished the song all of them were shedding tears, which I wondered at for not knowing the reason. When they were through singing they handed me the rattles and by signs asked me also to sing. I took the rattles and, to please them, began to sing to them the "Abado" (although they would not understand it), to which they were most attentive and indicated that it pleased them.

    Their chieftain was called Sumu, the second chieftain, Jausos; the others, Supitacse; Tilacse; Mutnc; Legeacse; Guecpostole; Xacacse.

For a worker in song

Leonard Cohen 1934-2016

      The shade just gets wetter
here birds aren't
                trying too hard not much noise
          from the oaks & their shadows

      The man who sang You got away
got away a lot later his voice
         only growls now
    in loops already made
loosening like shoelaces
        as I walk

              At canyon bottom Leona
    creek replaces itself
        with itself   Giant
    laurels angle & weave
                    Words
a man from between the wars wrote
        with holes so you could feel
    their heat give
        in the dark
follow me

        Here slopes of broken
    branch litter dense leaves
leaning countlessly
        downhill for love which is
    in this case sunlight

Leona Canyon Tr.

Infinity approximates as a canyonful of leaves

The   I just counted   12
        power lines belly across
    bird cries   What have I
done today

            Milk-top   shade-bottomed
      clouds stray southward
Tufts blow around   evaporating
          rain

         On the way home
                I'll stop   for hard-
    boiled eggs

Pine Tree Tr.

On waves

                  afternoon
upswells

      Sunlight on the underlying

    burdened body of salt

                    water begins

to disintegrate

                        Its ideas

    loosen & come

rippling   under low running

              branchcover on my

    creaky day

Caesar Chavez Park perimeter Tr.

On the hinge

                of a synapse: pillow talk.
Oceans of pavement painted like a holiday
with arrows & lines. In clinic waiting rooms
infomercials that go on to infinity.
Not ever wanting to wait:
flickers along dendrons, fractal. Pleated
line where you wait for the insides of you
& your luggage to be outlined

in tricolor. Linear equations, twinned
sweep of wiper blades. Axons give us
Antwerp, gargoyles, sun-faded
prayer flags high in mountains. High
on a can of whipped cream, meaning
your ion channels are slurred. A hundred
movies at once in a fuselage propelled

over clouds. With an isotope
& avalanche photodiodes humans watch
electric somethings among neurons.
Leaning over what eludes: banjo
duets, balsamic. How many angels
on the head of a pin, monks supposedly
wondered, snow falling, Europe,
drafty stone rooms. "It is the most

complex system," he said pasting
discs, wires to my brain's bone
case, "we know of in the universe."
All the way from Australia, what her eyes
looked like as a night we floated in
rustled across an empty pool.

Gray matter, glial cells, miles
of myelin. Caste systems, scoring

of a game in which love equals
zero. Above the proscenium a body
suspended in a gesture
for wings. Third acts. Sixth
extinction. New York, New
Yorkers bedstand piled.
In sugar & tomato paste, unconsumed
tater tots. Heated spoon, hollow

needle-tip. Heroines weaving shaped
sheet metal through the detail
of everyone else's cars. Dream
of speed where laws of speed
don't apply. In the colony, famine
imposed by men whose plates
are buttery with potatoes. A host

of angels, as in imagination,
dancing on pin-tip. I wake in the dark
to speed twenty minutes later
through a submarine tunnel. Dream
being also a performance
of neurons. This nothing of cobbled
alphabet. Dream of a shyly shining text,

almost as good as the look
in years ago eyes. Within each
skull, blood vessels go
100,000 miles. Like a light

rain drizzle or wind shivering
tree crowns, electrochemical pulses
past count. Cage fighting, a lost

umbrella, lit numbers diminishing
in a box on a pole. Neuroreceptors
aglow in the dopamine netting of love.
One too many blows
& the wheeling pulses may
wobble. About the pin & angels,

monks may never actually
have asked. As her scalpel draws
skin open, she is humming. Bugs
Bunny. Schooner, sails gusseted,
sailing around Cape Hope. Spoon.

What's my

        exit strategy   Just a bag
of senses on two legs   Half-buried bottle
      in pine needles   a rusting
tow hitch to my right
        Real wind wavering
in trees   Thought wind
     coming almost
to a pause

      Above the raggedy
patch city spreading
      into its blue bay on fire
oh for even
     shallow sleep

         The sky turns
its back on us but we
      can't tell because it's
        also blue

Side Hill Tr.

Whose woods

August 24, 1775

around me

                rattles   shedding

                        the reason

they   handed me

                        to

         understand   they were

Their chieftain was   the second   Jausos

others

                          Guecpostole

Bounced back no forwarding

After a helicopter you can
    almost hear the spiderwebs
glinting   one hammer
    dog bark   that big
pine fell downhill

Has imagination
    left here
a skyful of blue
      driverless
cars one after another going
    to a pileup of silence
& then a thousand
    scissoring birds

Skyline Ridge Tr.

How much fire

But what about the electric guitar? What if no walls
of amps warm & humming, no hand cradling strangely
tender feedback? My day begins in the dark,

coastline train-clatter, two more blocks of uncolored
pavement. Imagine life without it: days
like a sidewalk. Oh Richmond benzene, Richmond

mercury. How in a hundred you spent down for us
a hundred million summers. Your stills, your condensers.
Stove coils glowed on hills looking out on you, asphaltum,

grease, pale: words we didn't want to know. Where saltwater
marshes had rustled, ducks greened & speckled "in myriads,"
men sent from oil found abandoned ranches, a deep enough

bay, rails terminating. They zipped up your neck Richmond,
cast iron miles of pipe, mountains of copper for the three-
phasing current that your agitators might shake. Benzol,

zylol for dynamite. Highways unfurled, oceans overnighted,
from towers rippled wavelengths. New kinds of tones
blued off a Fender neck, fuzzed, trembled our car doors. Today

the 11th of February will be fifteen degrees

too warm. A train will go by where for a wage
I drag metal-clad cable into walls, airhorn drawing out

the bawl of progress. As it burns through you: swollen hulls
I always try not to see nesting at the shoreline north
of my life. Richmond polycyclic aromatic hydrocarbons

tucked into the wind, could I gauze what was missing
with headphones? Molecules catalytic-cracked to gasoline,
we drove away miles by the thousands, jetted them back.

Your tankers chuffed under the bridge. From your white-coated
work weeks sprang para-xylene for nylons, our skin was surprised,
phenol for glue to ply our plywoods. Houses sprawled,

you continued to do 300,000 barrels a day. Rivers

of kerosene to Bombay, Hanoi, nowhere too far. Oh city
that bore Standard Oil into the Pacific, tanker cars
clacked in before you had a city hall: Richemont,

by sword your name from a Norman hilltown to English castles
by gun to us. Every year a million pounds of heavy metals
into your air, onto Castro Cove's sludge-bottom. Chevroned

gulls wheel in our choices. Their lack. In my ears,
notes a magnet drew from wires flumed like schools
of fish. Richmond how would we be without you,

our hospitals' constant hum, shimmer of components spirited
from everywhere to our thumbs. On a carpet of carbon
flying. I stepped down from something diesel

to search bins for the sound of *anger & queen jealousy, Bold
as Love,* driven through tubing. Out of vinyl flaring, fingers

of Jimi Hendrix, about to swallow too much fire.

Are you coming to the farewell party

        Rust-colored redwood
              leaflets   now I only
have a sex-life   on the inside
        Did you go
     to the window & slide it
              shut   The rains
went on & I was kind of
            ruins people visited
    later

                   When those last
    11 birds go back
      inside the serrated
edges of their calls
        & the wind rides through
in machines   that burn wind
   we can put our glass
        maps to sleep   hungry & go

play cards in a hall
    full of empty
        folding tables

Palos Colorados Tr.

Brain-ache at San Leandro Creek

pay health insurance
    pick up both kinds
of milk   try again for bank
    to stop phantom auto-transfer
listen to the creek drizzle
    over stones   under the dense
bay canopy   can't
    do much but close
sore eyes

Skyline Ridge Tr. Via Huckleberry

Poem for a watershed
with found objects

Foam scum near an overpass
& an egret. Does a steelhead
still pause? Down-bank
shopping cart someone

shoved. Dear Wildcat Creek,

what happened to you
after you stayed for our 20th century
dams, sand trucked in,

a few dollars' soft serve? Laked,
you bent on through laurel
alleys, along amble-y pastureland

you worked on your rocks.
Under soiling leaves,
our smudged foil
wrappers forever. San Pablo,

Richmond grew uphill,
you went under double exes
of Food Maxx, two freeways.

Can I still get to know you,

already saying goodbye, my steps
on your September dry bed.

"It's like that," said the man
with a bucket, "all the way
to Three Bells." Bike frame,

moldy half-coconut. Queen
boxspring on its side on stones
from a million years. In this state

fifty places had Wildcat
tacked to them. Peel that

back & you were *Arroyo Seco*
also *Chiquito* & before that
how many ways did they

say you? Names with saved
souls ground into dirt
floors Franciscans called the Sending

of Sorrows. Now who gives the ten
thousand thank yous, dragonfly's

blue buzz, sack of birdseed,
ivy whispering behind closed

faces of fences. All over a culvert,
spray-paint riots on lime-
hardened gray. Is this

where you end below the rumble
of Chevron's processes.

Upside-down industrial
mop bucket, laundry
on a line by another

tarp tent.
One white ski.

Whose woods

                                                      August 24, 1775

                      by me

                                the song   *of*

          not knowing   *When*

I   *took*

               please   *the Abado*

pleased

           Sumu Jausos

the others

Could I

        throw my city away
     like packaging if
            only for hours
   From above it was
      haze-bed   road-hatch
        dopplering

My friends had begun dying
      or receded

   to a den to be involved in
      glass & complicated light
           Immune systems moving
away from us   inflammation seeped
   in windows we didn't
      know opened

  Still I climbed a sheer
rock-strewn trail   lookout to grid spread
    unremitted
        four-stroke motors also by the minute
    devouring
          Old Tunnel Road

Sungreen pieces   of shade in their
      wind fanned   millions
           Could I be a little
       less me   or more leaf

   My city was not bothered it had time
by the throat

Side Hill Tr.

Greenness with picnic bench

Train steam the size
of five year olds looping
through laurels, family
swarmed lake, your algae
deepening, ash-piles

of after-coals.
Did you see the Pacific
tree frog's skin
fall off from zoospores
that rode in on a distant
new year's
bullfrogs? Sorry

you were eucaplyptused,
sloppily pined. Your footpaths
spring back with red-happy
hazard plants

so one more for falling

leafcover: Tilden good

bye hello, time
a tiny bit softer, meadow

waving, bathrooms
slab damp, roads
sliding through you,
marginal newts crossing.

I can't say you
enough, cloud rustle,

bluejay branch, window
to under cities.

Grass come waist
high in places,
little spoon leaves
stay one more day.

Hill waltz
with crow calls, alien
green golf course we lean
so hard on you: bark

shag stray feather
the uttering after all
our wearing on it
of Wildcat Creek

Note on the poems

Forest bathing, I was told, is a Japanese term for immersing in environments where the visual field to the peripheries is uniformly rich, to support the brain's healing.

For months following a car accident, while I was unable to process light and sound normally, I spent day after day hiking trails of shorelines and woods in the hills that overlook the East Bay Area. In my pack I carried lunch, nature guides, a mat for napping, and a notebook (and sometimes a copy of Hass's *The Essential Haiku*).

After I had recovered, working through my forest-bathing notebooks, I felt a need to see past the surface layer of these parklands, their strata in the current moment. What did they look like before European colonization, when they were home of the Lisjan (Ohlone) peoples? The available sources are texts of the first European explorers: work documents of the employees of empires, assessing property—potential or claimed. I culled passages that offered glimpses.

I found a way to recover from my concussion. Injuries to the land continue to unfold. The Lisjan (Ohlone) work steadily toward their vision of rematriation, "Indigenous women-led work to restore sacred relationships between Indigenous people and our ancestral land," including the recovery of the Chochechnyo language and traditional culture. I offer this to the possibility of recoveries.

Sources

Fray Vicente Santa Maria, *The first Spanish entry into San Francisco Bay*
Georg Heinrich Langsdorf, *Voyages and travels in various parts of the world 1803-7*
Father Juan Crespi, *Journals of the exploration of 1699*
Frederick W. Beechy, *Narrative of a Voyage to the Pacific and Beering's Staights in 1825-28*
George Vancouver, *A Voyage of Discovery to the North Pacific Ocean and round the world*
Robert Hass, *The Essential Haiku: Versions of Basho, Buson, and Issa*

For resources on healing concussion and many other types of brain maladies, see:
Norman Doidge, *The Brain's Way of Healing*

To learn about and support the rematriation work of the Lisjan (Ohlone) people, visit https://sogoreate-landtrust.org/.

Acknowledgments

"Across grazing hills," *The Dodge* April 2024
"Are you going to the farewell party," *Palaver* Spring 2020
"Bounced back no forwarding," *Palaver* Spring 2020
"Because my father got a better job," *Zyzzyva* Spring 2023
"Greenness with Picnic Bench," *Star82* September 2019
"Off trail," *Angel Rust* August 2021
"On the hinge," *Parhelion* October 2023
"Poem in blue with the news," *Hamilton Stone* 2021
"Poem for a watershed with found objects," *Parhelion* October 2023
"Stony trail, visibility nil," *Parhelion* October 2023
"Wind Opens Me Closed," *Angel Rust* August 2021
"Who goes," *Hamilton Stone* 2021
"You Sleep," *Angel Rust* August 2021

Title Index

A
Across grazing hills 50
Are you coming to the farewell party 70

B
Because my father got a better job 26
Birds I don't know 57
Blue 23
Bounced back no forwarding 67
Brain-ache at San Leandro Creek 71
Butterfly hidden in hills color 14

C
Chaparral ("the understory") 31
Could I 75

D
David won't call me from his car anymore 48
Days unshowered 34
Does the bay 55

E
Every day the same 33

F
For a worker in song 59

G
Greenness with picnic bench 36, 76

H
Hills full of holes 56
How can I 53
How much fire 68

I
I fell 13
In a last 25
Infinity approximates as a canyonful of leaves 60
In the middle of 20

M
Manzanita barren 49

N
No returns 15

O
Ode to fMRI (the Cure) 42
Off trail 30
On the hinge 62
On waves 61

P
Poem for a watershed with found objects 72
Poem in blue with the news 40
Poem with time & mildly injured brain 21

R
Ripples 28

S
Stony trail, visibility nil 46
Sweet little 18

T
Taking cane 16

W

Westward Frank C Havens 17
"What fish feel" 41
What's my 65
Who goes 29
Whose woods 19, 24, 32, 35, 39, 44, 47, 51, 52, 58, 66, 74
Wind opens me closed 12

Y

You said 22
You sleep 38

First Line Index

Symbol
& this is for the core, bathed 42

A
After a helicopter you can 67
afternoon 61
a hundred & some years 26
a lot of sky 20
apart on a little wind 13
around me 66
At this cove ... there is a rancheria of Indians,
    who came out from 39

B
besides the many good-sized cottonwoods
    on the river, there 52
Birdcall a doorlatch 12
branch rustle 33
busy pin-flies 34
But what about the electric guitar?
    What if no walls 68
by me 74

C
corner brown 25
Coyote brush 31

E
Elaborate gnat & dapple, O Tilden 36
Even if it's not 40
exit strategy Just a bag 65

F
far we entered 35
Foam scum near an overpass 72
Fog pours 46
forgive us Giant-banked 55

H
highborn of Sag Harbor came 17

I
in a cold ocean 41
into the dry dry 29
I tumbled almost 30
It was then a perfect calm,
   and in a very fine morning we 47
I went into the outlet store 15

L
Lazing in striations 48
like a robot wind 50

O
O common buckeye on the ground 14
of a synapse: pillow talk 62
of twisty 16
of wild 24

P
pay health insurance 71

R
Rust-colored redwood 70

S

sing the misery whip, a man at each end
  as its crosscut teeth tore 53
so craving for 51
Spidery night: sleep webby day laced with thinner 21
sun blaring my eyes 23
switchback 18

T

The I just counted 12 60
their calls 57
The number of wild geese ...
  is quite extraordinary, and indeed 19
there were no more 22
The shade just gets wetter 59
the wind hollows it is 56
They all crowded around me and,
  sitting by me, began to sing 58
throw my city away 75
Train steam the size 76

W

We had not proceeded far from this
  delightful spot, when we entered 32
where water skeeters paddle 28
who came shouting 44
with bird-seeded 49
with our daughter 38

www.ingramcontent.com/pod-product-compliance
Lightning Source LLC
Chambersburg PA
CBHW010046090426
42735CB00020B/3408